MAMMOTH CAVE
NATIONAL PARK

by Ruth Radlauer

Photographs
by Ed Radlauer

Design and map
by Rolf Zillmer

AN ELK GROVE BOOK

CHILDRENS PRESS®
CHICAGO

Photo Credits:
Cave Research Foundation, page 31
Clark, Chip, page 27 (bottom)
R. Cetera, cover, pages 9, 41 (top)
Payl Hayes, pages 17 (bottom), 23
Mammoth Cave National Park, pages 5, (frog),
19 (salamander), 33 (top right),
41 (bottom right), 42 (top), 42 (bottom),
43 (bottom)
Smithsonian Institute, 25 (top)

Cover photo: Travertine In Frozen Niagara

Library of Congress Cataloging in Publication Data

Radlauer, Ruth Shaw.
  Mammoth Cave National Park.
  (Parks for people)
  "An Elk Grove book."
  SUMMARY: Discusses the rock formations, animal
life, vegetation, and history of the world's longest
cave.
  1. Mammoth Cave National Park—Juvenile literature.
[1. Mammoth Cave National Park. 2. Caves. 3. Na-
tional parks and reserves] I. Radlauer, Edward.
II. Zillmer, Rolf. III. Title.
F457.M2R25   976.9'754   77-26764
ISBN 0-516-07496-2

11 12 13 14 15 R 92 91 90 89 88

Contents

What is Mammoth Cave National Park?

Mammoth Cave National Park is a hilly place covered with trees. You could hike and hike and never know you were walking over the longest cave in the world.

Mammoth Cave can be a short walk through narrow passages to Frozen Niagara, where minerals have formed what looks like a waterfall turned to stone.

This park is a long guided walk through a historic cave from which a mineral was taken to make gunpowder for the War of 1812. On the Historic Tour, the guides may have you stand still while they turn off the lights. Then Mammoth Cave becomes the sight of total darkness and the sound of total silence.

Outside the cave, this park is the sound of many kinds of birds and a night chorus of frogs.

Inside the cave are crickets, bats, blindfish, and white crayfish. Do you suppose they are waiting for you to come and explore their deep, dark world 100 meters under the ground?

Good Spring Trail

Drapery Room—Frozen Niagara

Rotunda Room

Frog

Your Trip to Mammoth Cave

Mammoth Cave National Park is in south-central Kentucky. You can drive there from Louisville, Kentucky, or Nashville, Tennessee, on Interstate 65. Some people stop just long enough to take one or two guided cave tours. Others stay at the hotel or in cottages.

You may want to stay in the campground where each site has a fireplace, table, and benches. Nearby are restrooms and running water.

The most important thing you can take to Mammoth Cave is a sense of wondering, or curiosity. Curiosity, mixed with a pair of good walking shoes or hiking boots, will make your trip an adventure. Besides nature trails and a river, there are many cave trails to explore with the park technicians who guide all tours.

With strong legs, lots of energy, and plenty of questions, you'll gather a long list of discoveries at Mammoth Cave National Park.

Write to the Superintendent, Mammoth Cave National Park, Mammoth Cave, Kentucky 42259, for information to help you plan your trip.

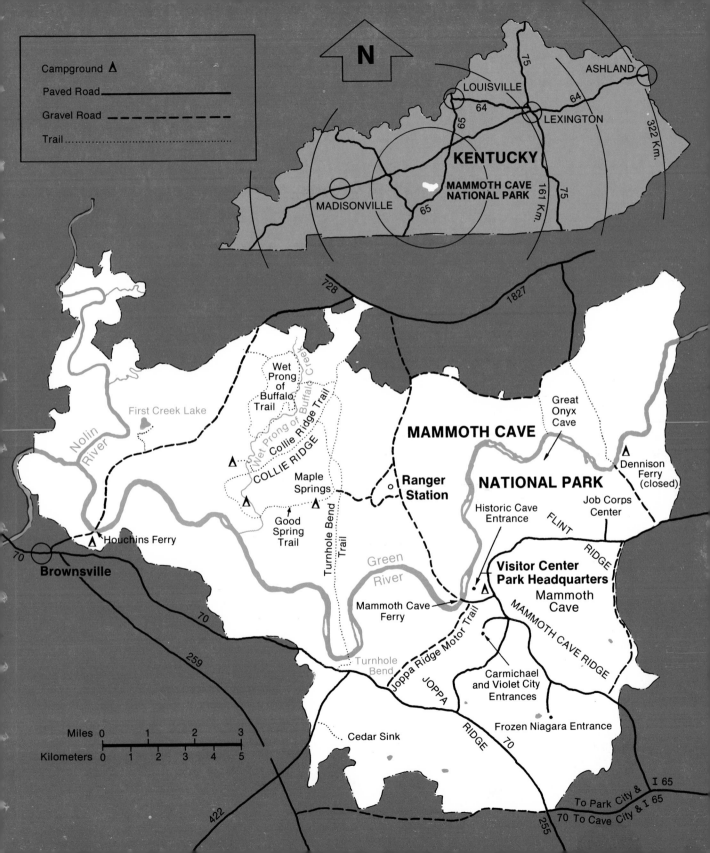

Before the Cave

Two hundred and fifty million years! That's a long time, but it has taken that long to bring about the caves in Mammoth Cave National Park.

About that long ago, a shallow inland sea covered this area. For millions of years animals lived and died in that sea. As they died their shells and bones settled in layers of slimy ooze on the bottom of the sea.

Sand and mud washed into the sea, and they settled in layers too. The layers became so thick that the weight squeezed out the water. This cemented all the sediments together to form solid rock. The shells and ooze became limestone. The mud became shale, and sand turned into sandstone.

In ages that followed, the sea dried up and filled again many times. During this time limestone, sandstone, and shale collected until the layers were about 900 meters thick.

When forces within the earth moved, the land rose very slowly and the sea disappeared. The uplift tilted the rocks, and they cracked and warped, or bent.

Layers Laid Down In An Inland Sea ▶

The Work of Water

After the inland sea had gone, heavy rains fell and rivers flowed across the land. Wind and water wore away many layers of sedimentary rock.

For about 30 million years the Green River has slowly worn its way down through sandstone to the limestone layers. As the water flowed over the land, it picked up acid from decaying plants. Following underground cracks, this slightly acid water dissolved the limestone and carried it away in liquid form. This cut passages through the limestone. Water continued to flow there for many years, making the openings bigger and bigger.

By about one million years ago, the Green River had cut a canyon, or gorge. Then the underground water could drain out of the openings into the gorge. Slowly the water level dropped. As the water level fell, the limestone passages were left drained and dry.

This is how the Mammoth area got the four things needed to form caves: water, rocks with cracks in them, rock like limestone that dissolves, and a place for the water to drain.

Green River, Brown From Heavy Rain

Limestone Passage Drained And Dry

Cave Formations

Mammoth Cave is covered by hills, or ridges. Water flows down these ridges and seeps through the thinner soil at the base of the ridge. As it goes through soil, water picks up carbonic acid. Seeping down through rocks, the carbonic acid dissolves calcium carbonate out of the limestone layer. As water slowly drips into the cave through a small ceiling hole, the calcium carbonate forms a ring around the hole. More drips of water bring more of this mineral. The ring gets longer and becomes a tube much like a soda straw. Water keeps trickling through the tube which then becomes a stalactite.

After a long time, the tube closes, so water flows down the outsides of the soda straw. Then the stalactite takes on a new and interesting shape.

Sometimes water seeps through longer cracks in the cave ceiling, and the calcium carbonate forms sheets that look like curtains or draperies.

For some unknown reason, another strange shape forms when the calcium carbonate builds out in all directions to make wiggly shapes called helictites.

Stalactites—Onyx Cave

Soda Straws And Drapery—Frozen Niagara Tour

More Cave Formations

Collections, or deposits, of calcium carbonate are called travertine. When drops of water fall on the floor of a cave, the travertine builds into a mound. The mound of travertine gets taller and taller and forms a stalagmite.

You can remember the names of these formations if you remember the *c* in stala*c*tite on the *c*eiling and the *g* in the stalag*mite* on the *g*round. You can also remember that the stala*ctite* holds *tight* to the ceiling, and the stalag*mite might* stay on the ground.

When a stalactite and a stalagmite meet, they become a pillar or column.

If water seeps down the side of a cave and travertine builds out from the wall, it makes flowstone.

Most formations take hundreds of years to grow as big as the ones in Mammoth Cave.

Many kilometers of Mammoth Cave passages are dry and without formations. But you will see many of these strange travertine shapes when you visit Frozen Niagara or Great Onyx Cave.

Stalagmites—Onyx Cave

Stalactites (Left) And Flowstone (Center)

Gypsum

In dryer parts of the cave, wetness seeps through cave walls and deposits a softer mineral called gypsum. Gypsum may build up between rock layers and push them apart.

In other places, crystals of gypsum build up around a center to form a blister called a snowball. As more and more gypsum forces its way through the center of the snowball, it bursts open into a lovely "feather" or "flower."

Crystals of gypsum build into many different shapes. Some grow into spikes as thin as thread.

Gypsum is an important mineral. When it's heated, gypsum becomes a fine white powder of many uses. The powder is used to make plaster of paris, paint, and plaster board.

On the Half-day Tour, you can see gypsum formations at the Snowball Room, in Alice's Grotto, and on the Mammoth Wall.

Gypsum Flower

Gypsum Flowers

Who Lives in a Cave?

Some animals like to visit caves. They live above ground, but often find shelter in caves. Since they only visit, they are called trogloxenes, or "cave guests." Mammoth Cave has about 15 kinds of trogloxenes, including bats, crickets, and some salamanders.

A bat can find its way in the darkness outside or in a cave. As it flies, the bat makes a very high-pitched squeak we cannot hear. When this squeak bounces off an object, the bat hears an echo. By the echo, a bat can judge how far away an object is and dodge it or catch it.

Some other animals like to live in dark, wet places. These are troglophiles, or "lovers of caves." Troglophiles in Mammoth are some kinds of spiders, crickets, beetles, and other insects. The cave salamander is also a troglophile.

The troglophile cricket does not chirp as surface crickets do, and its antennae, or feelers, are longer than its body. Most cave crickets go to the surface to feed when the climate outside is as dark, damp, and cool as a cave.

Bat—A trogloxene

Salamander—A Troglophile

Cave Cricket—A Troglophile

Troglobites

Troglobites live their whole lives inside caves. They will die if something like a flood forces them out. About 27 kinds of troglobites live in Mammoth Cave. There are millipedes, flatworms, and six kinds of beetles.

Two troglobites, living on the lowest level of Mammoth Cave in the Echo River, are the white crayfish and the blindfish.

The white crayfish moves through the water very slowly, waving its long antennae to find what food there is in the water.

The blindfish also moves very slowly. With each stroke of its fins, it travels farther than a surface fish would. Without turning, it goes for long distances in search of flatworms and tiny floating matter called plankton. By using small sensors on its head, the blindfish finds food. But since there is very little food in the Echo River, this troglobite is only about the size of your finger.

White Crayfish

Blindfish

Sunshine and "Trogs"

How can all these "trogs" live in a cave? How can there be life without sunshine?

Believe it or not, the sun's energy is very important to a cave. Plants above the cave use the sun's energy to make green leaves and grass. Some animals eat green plants and are eaten by other animals.

When animals and plants die, they decay and become a part of the soil called humus. Water washes part of the humus into caves where it serves as food for some cave animals. Then those cave animals, or even their droppings, become food for other cave life. When you go on a cave tour, you may get a chance to look for some of these "trogs": crickets, beetles, snails, and spiders.

Sunshine, also called solar energy, is even important to the making of caves. From living and dying things on earth's surface, water gets the weak acid needed to dissolve limestone and form caves.

Do you suppose the "trogs" know that, without sunshine, there would be no food or even a cave?

How Is Sunshine Important To A Cave?

Young Caver In White Cave

Looking For "Trogs"

People in Mammoth Cave

About 4000 years ago or more, an ancient people lived in this part of the country. Now called the Adena Indians, they may have found shelter in the cave entrances. But archeologists, the scientists who study the works of ancient people, believe the Adenas may have explored the cave without living in it.

Woven sandals, cane sticks burned for torches, and wooden bowls have been found in the cave. They tell us that some people explored almost five kilometers into the cave.

By other signs, we know the Adena Indians scraped gypsum from walls of the cave. Archeologists believe they may have used gypsum to make paint. The Indians also may have thought gypsum had magic powers.

In 1935 some guides discovered the body of an ancient gypsum miner. Wedged under a huge boulder, the body had dried out and looked like a mummy.

Later the boulder was lifted and moved so scientists could study the body. They wanted to discover more about these people who first explored Mammoth Cave.

Adena Indian

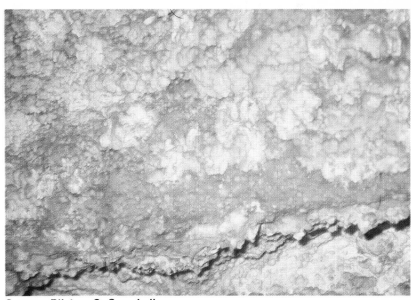

Gypsum Blisters Or Snowballs

Cave Guides and Explorers

Mammoth Cave was unknown to the first Kentucky settlers. One legend says the cave was discovered in 1799 when a hunter chased a bear into the Historic Entrance.

In 1838 the cave was owned by Franklin Gorin, whose black slave, Stephen Bishop, was a guide. Visitors enjoyed the way he explained this "grand, gloomy, and peculiar" place. He explored parts of the cave where few had gone. He discovered the Echo River and found its blindfish. After the cave was sold to a doctor, Bishop found Mammoth Dome, the Snowball Room, and other places. He drew a fairly accurate map of Mammoth Cave.

In 1908, his grandnephew, Ed Bishop, guided a German visitor who made a more accurate map. They discovered Bishop's Pit, Kaemper Hall, and Violet City.

People from everywhere came to explore. Some paid extra to build rock monuments or to write their names on walls and ceilings. *But that was before the cave was in a national park and protected from changes made by people.*

Private Person's Monument, 1928

Follow The Guide

A Tourist Attraction

When Dr. John Croghan bought Mammoth Cave from Mr. Gorin, he made the hotel bigger and improved the roads. Guides were very busy taking people through this popular tourist attraction.

But Dr. Croghan wanted to experiment with a cure for tuberculosis. He built wooden and stone huts in the cave so his patients could live in a constant temperature of around 12° celsius. The experiment failed, and Dr. Croghan himself died of tuberculosis.

Sometimes, on a lantern tour, you may see the stone huts and some places discovered by Bishop and others. Past the stone huts you light the lanterns provided by the park. Then you go by lantern light up hills, through narrow passages, and along wide avenues.

You'll see where early visitors made monuments of rocks and where they wrote their names with smoke from candles.

At one place you can follow an easy dirt path or choose to walk over the rocks of the Old Guides' Trail. The big flat rocks make hollow clomping sounds as each slab tips back and forth under the weight of your steps.

Lantern Tour

Old Guides' Trail

The Longest Cave

Stephen Bishop began a long history of exploring and discovery. Pete Hanson and Lee Hunt made new discoveries 100 years later. Others looked for new caves in the Flint Ridge area east of Mammoth Cave Ridge. In 1895 Lute and Henry Lee found Colossal Cave, and Edmund Turner discovered Great Onyx Cave in 1915. Floyd Collins found Crystal Cave and died exploring a cave by himself.

Some cavers believed Crystal Cave was the longest cave in the world. In 1953 a private group of people began a long project of mapping the caves. They also hoped to connect Mammoth Cave with the Flint Ridge caves.

Later organized as the Cave Research Foundation, these people struggled for years to find connections. On September 9, 1972, a group of five men and one woman found the connection between the lower end of Hanson's Lost River and the Echo River in Mammoth. This made the surveyed part of the Flint Mammoth Cave System about 232 kilometers long, the longest known cave in the world. It is now more than 321 kilometers in length.

Hanson's Lost River ▶

To Know a Cave

If you want to explore a cave, you can visit Mammoth Cave any time of year. But different cave tours are offered at different times and seasons. You should be in very good condition to go on most cave tours.

A Historic Tour takes you on a two-hour round trip. In the great Rotunda Room, you see huge vats where cave soil was soaked to take out a mineral used to make gunpowder. In the 1800s, water was piped into the vats through hollow logs of tulip trees. You can cross the Bottomless Pit, squeeze through Fat Man's Misery, and see the Ruins of Karnak.

The shortest tour is Frozen Niagara. You'll see wet and dry passages and many kinds of travertine formations. The Half-day Tour is a harder hike. For the Wild Cave Tour, you must be at least 16 and in very good condition. You'll have to work your way through passages barely big enough for a very large person to inch through.

You buy tickets for all cave trips at the Visitor Center where tours and times are posted.

Pipes Made From Tulip Tree—Historic Tour

Frozen Niagara

Wild Cave Tour

Caving on Wheels

Even people who can't walk get to see Mammoth Cave. How? By caving on wheels. Sometimes groups of people get together to arrange wheelchair tours. Or a family can ask for a tour. Every person in a chair needs someone to push because the trails are bumpy.

Wheel cavers need their own bus or cars for the short trip from the Visitor Center to the entrance. A park guide rides along to show the way. Then an elevator takes everyone down more than 81 meters to the Snowball Room.

If you take this tour, you'll go through a tube passage called Cleaveland Avenue. Before you wheel back to the Snowball Room, you'll see gypsum flowers.

Then you can explore a short way along Boone Avenue if you like. At the beginning of a narrow canyon passage, you can see cave grapes. These are bits of travertine shaped like popcorn.

To get the real cave experience, ask your guide to turn off the lights. What do you think you'll see and hear?

This 1½-hour tour ends with a ride back up the elevator.

Touring Mammoth Cave On Wheels

From Forest to Farms to Forest

If you came to Kentucky to settle in the 1800s, you found a country covered with trees.

Using the tall, straight trunks of the tulip tree, or yellow poplar, you helped your family build a house and barn. You built them on a ridge above the river. Then when the river flooded, it left mud and silt along the banks. This made good fertile land for crops.

Today the farms of Mammoth Cave area have disappeared. When farmers left the land, it went through some changes we call succession.

First the fields turned to grass and weeds where grasshoppers and sparrows lived. Slowly shrubs and small cedars took root, and rabbits, red foxes, and skunks came for shelter. As the cedars grew tall, they shaded young deciduous trees, the kind that drop their leaves in the fall. Gray foxes, white-tailed deer, and owls and other birds liked this kind of habitat, or home.

By the end of about 70 years of plant and animal succession, the farm fields had turned into deciduous forests where many animals found habitats.

Deciduous Forest ▶

Animals

Today you can walk the trails of Mammoth Cave National Park and see who lives here now. If you get out early and move quietly, you may see gray squirrels, white-tail deer, or a big pileated woodpecker with a crest on its head. Another crested bird to see is the blue jay, a noisy bird that seems to squawk for attention.

Walking at night, you may see raccoons that come down from their tree homes to beg. But if you go out after dark, be sure to shine a flashlight on the path. Another animal, the beautiful but poisonous copperhead snake, likes to lie on paving that's still warm from the daytime sun.

Copperheads also come out at night to feed on insects, mice, and other rodents. When daylight comes, the copperhead curls up and hides where its patterned skin blends with the brown leaves. It hardly moves all day as it waits for night to return.

You'll be safe from this reptile's poisonous bite if you stay in the middle of the trail and always watch where you step.

Blue Jay

Raccoon

Copperhead

Wild Flowers

Alone or on a nature walk, you can stroll through a thick forest. Hickory, oak, maple, ash, and cedar trees shelter many flowering plants. A park naturalist points out the many wild flowers along the trail.

In open, sunny places, the orange blooms of butterfly weed dazzle your eyes. The naturalist says this plant is named for the insects that are drawn to its bright blossoms.

During the spring your guide shows you Jack-in-the-pulpit, hidden among other shade-loving plants. From April to June, Jack-in-the-pulpit blooms with a tube that seems to shelter a "Jack" in its center. The "Jack" turns into red fruit by late summer. Indians used to boil or bake its turniplike root. Then they dried and pounded it to make flour. The flour was heated again and left to stand until it was mild enough to eat.

If people eat this "Indian turnip" raw, it causes a stinging pain in the mouth for a long time. But some animals can eat the leaves and red berries of Jack-in-the-pulpit.

Butterfly Weed

Blossom Of Jack-In-The-Pulpit

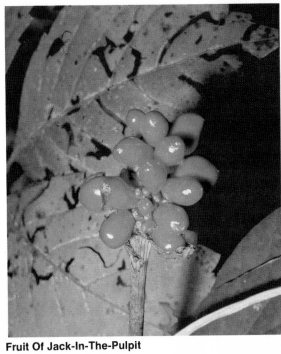

Fruit Of Jack-In-The-Pulpit

The Backcountry

Besides going in caves, you can enjoy the river when you take a cruise on Miss Green River II. Or if you have a canoe, you can camp anywhere on islands or along the banks. You can fish without a license, but ask at Park Headquarters about catch limits. The Green River may look peaceful, but it's full of hidden dangers and swift currents, so swimming is not a good idea.

As with canoe camping, backpackers need backcountry use permits. North of the Green River, there are almost 42 kilometers of horse and hiking trails. The Good Spring Trail makes a 16-kilometer loop past three campsites with fire rings. You can only burn downed and dead wood, which is hard to find, so a backpacker's stove should go into your pack along with drinking water.

Good day hikes are on Turnhole and Collie Ridges and on the Wet Prong of the Buffalo loop. You sign your name in a box at the beginning of these trails. Be sure to let someone know where you're going and when you'll return. On any hike, you need extra water, emergency food, and a first aid kit. Then stay on trails to avoid snakes and ticks.

Miss Green River II

Backpackers Need Permits

Cave Magic

As you hike the trails of this park, you might think about how the sun's energy is important to the cave. Without sun there would be no plants or animals on the surface. Animals give off a gas called carbon dioxide. Falling raindrops gather some of that gas. When added to water, carbon dioxide becomes carbonic acid.

Without the sun's energy there would be no humus from which water gets a little more acid. Carbonic acid in water dissolves calcium carbonate out of the limestone. And it's the calcium carbonate that turns into the travertine of stalactites, stalagmites, and other wondrous shapes.

When it rains, you can crawl into your tent and wonder about water dripping into the cave. What shape will it form out of the travertine it deposits?

Water has decorated the caves for millions of years. Will it go on forever? Who knows? But as long as water falls from Kentucky skies, it will find its way below the surface. And there it will work its underground magic in Mammoth Cave National Park.

Underground Magic

Other National Parks in the East

ACADIA NATIONAL PARK includes islands and a peninsula on the coast of Maine. Here, rounded granite mountains show the passage of a glacier that melted between 12,000 and 15,000 years ago. Deep enough to cover a range of mountains, the glacier carved basins where many lakes and a fjord now reflect the blue of cool summer skies.

Autumn colors and spring flowers bring visitors from all over the world to GREAT SMOKY MOUNTAINS NATIONAL PARK. Some of the homes and farms of early settlers in Tennessee and North Carolina are preserved as living history in this park.

EVERGLADES NATIONAL PARK is home for snakes, alligators, and other reptiles. It's a winter vacation in Florida for many kinds of birds, big and small. Mammals in this park include raccoons, panthers, and sea-going manatees.

Where Mountains Meet The Sea—Acadia National Park

Hardwood Forest—Great Smoky Mountains National Park

Get To Know A Snake—Everglades National Park

The Author and Illustrator

Wyoming-born Ruth Radlauer's love affair with national parks began in Yellowstone. During her younger years, she spent her summers in the Bighorn Mountains, in Yellowstone, or on Casper Mountain.

Ed and Ruth Radlauer, graduates of the University of California at Los Angeles, are authors of many books for young people. Along with their young adult daughter and sons, they photograph and write about a wide variety of subjects ranging from motorcycles to monkeys.

The Radlauers live in California, where Ruth and Ed spend most of their time in the mountains near Los Angeles.